I Am
Patient

by Sarah L. Schuette

Consulting Editor: Gail Saunders-Smith, Ph.D.

Consultant: Madonna Murphy, Ph.D.
Professor of Education,
University of St. Francis, Joliet, Illinois
Author, *Character Education in America's
Blue Ribbon Schools*

Pebble Books

an imprint of Capstone Press
Mankato, Minnesota

Pebble Books are published by Capstone Press
151 Good Counsel Drive, P.O. Box 669, Mankato, Minnesota 56002
http://www.capstone-press.com

1 2 3 4 5 6 07 06 05 04 03 02

Library of Congress Cataloging-in-Publication Data
Schuette, Sarah L., 1976–
    I am patient / by Sarah L. Schuette.
    p. cm.—(Character values)
    Includes bibliographical references and index.
    Summary: Simple text and photographs show various ways children can
be patient.
    ISBN 0-7368-1441-8 (hardcover)
    1. Patience—Juvenile literature. [1. Patience.] I. Title. II. Series.
BJ1533.P3 S38 2003
179′.9—dc21   2001008430

Note to Parents and Teachers

The Character Values series supports national social studies standards for units on individual development and identity. This book describes patience and illustrates ways students can be patient. The images support early readers in understanding the text. The repetition of words and phrases helps early readers learn new words. This book also introduces early readers to subject-specific vocabulary words, which are defined in the Words to Know section. Early readers may need assistance to read some words and to use the Table of Contents, Words to Know, Read More, Internet Sites, and Index/Word List sections of the book.

Table of Contents

I am patient. I can wait calmly.

I practice my
spelling words until
I know them better.
I keep trying.

I wait for my turn
to use the computer.

I wait patiently
for the bus.

I wait to speak until my teacher calls on me.

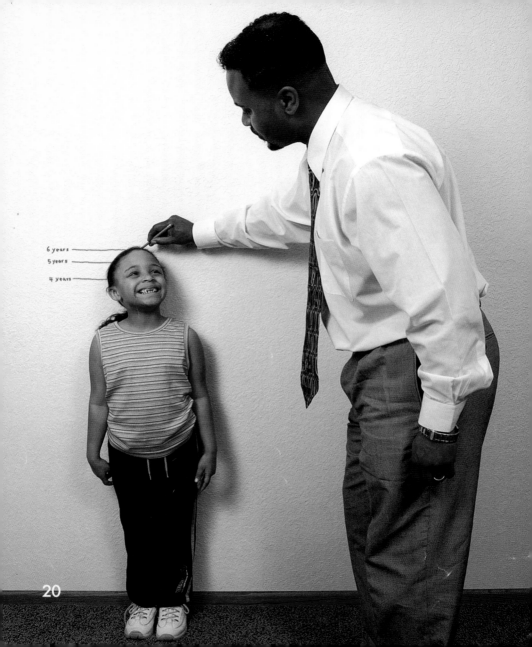

6 years
5 years
4 years

20

I am patient and calm.
I am not in a hurry. I
can wait.

Words to Know

angry—wanting to argue or fight with someone

calm—quiet and peaceful; patient people are calm while they wait for something.

hurry—to do things as fast as you can

listen—to pay attention so that you can hear something; people who are patient listen quietly until it is their turn to talk.

patient—waiting calmly without complaining; patient people do not get angry or upset when things do not go as they expect.

practice—to keep working to improve a skill

wait—to stay in a place or do nothing for a long time until something happens; patient people can wait calmly.

Read More

Kyle, Kathryn. *Patience.* Wonder Books. Chanhassen, Minn.: Child's World, 2002.

Lewis, Barbara. *Being Your Best: Character Building for Kids 7–10.* Minneapolis: Free Spirit, 2000.

Raatma, Lucia. *Patience.* Character Education. Mankato, Minn.: Bridgestone Books, 2000.

Internet Sites

Adventures from the Book of Virtues
http://pbskids.org/adventures

Character Counts National Home Page
http://www.charactercounts.org

Character Education: Free Resources for Teachers
http://www.goodcharacter.com

Index/Word List

Word Count: 102
Early-Intervention Level: 9

Editorial Credits
Mari C. Schuh, editor; Jennifer Schonborn, book designer and illustrator;
   Nancy White, photo stylist

Photo Credits
Capstone Press/Gary Sundermeyer, cover, 1, 4, 6, 8, 10, 20; Gregg Andersen, 12,
   14, 16, 18

Pebble Books thanks the Frederick family of North Mankato, Minnesota, for
modeling in this book.

The author dedicates this book to her parents, Willmar and Jane Schuette,
Belle Plaine, Minnesota.

24

t s i L d ʁ o w ʎ x ε ɩ